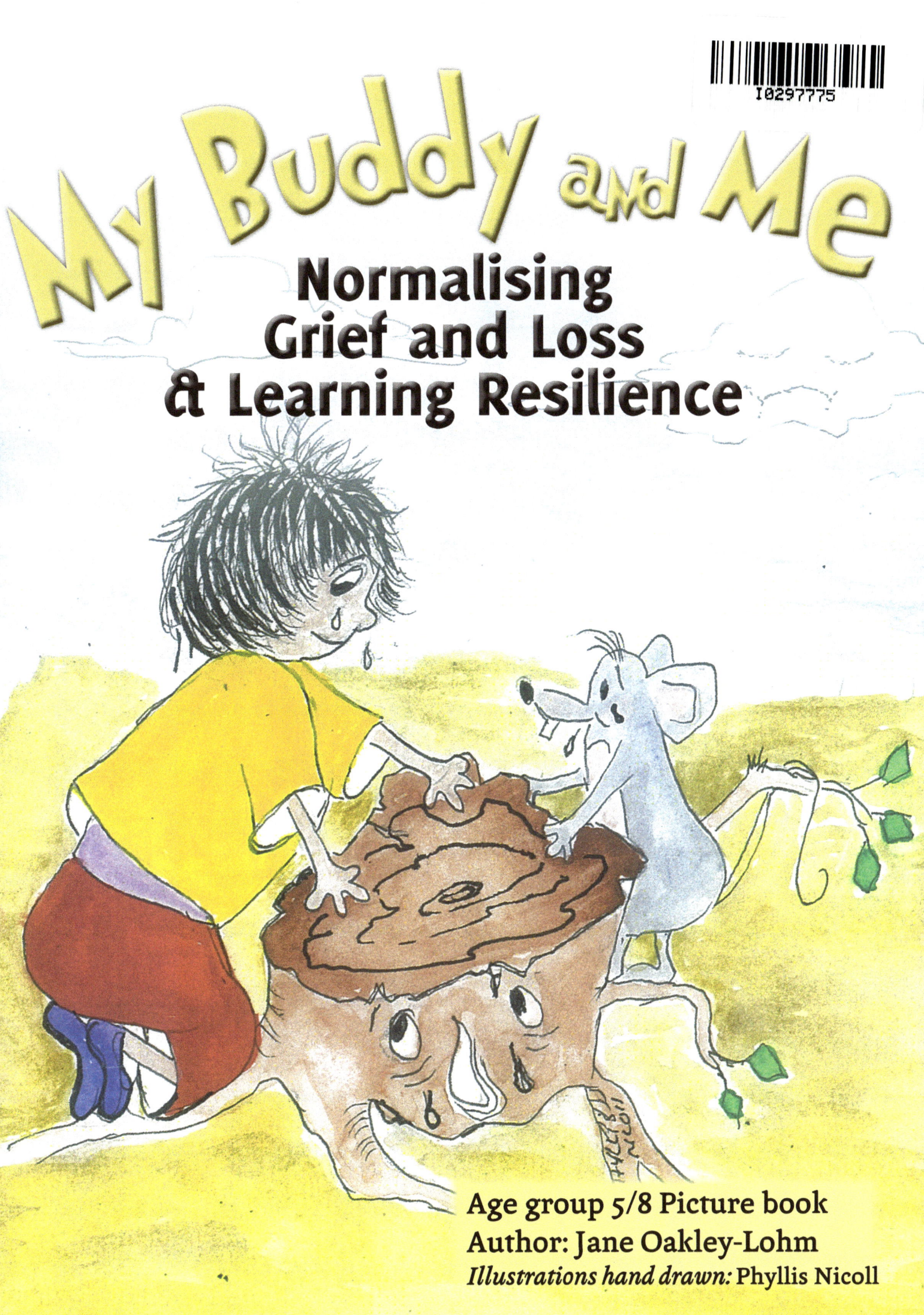

 A catalogue record for this book is available from the National Library of Australia

Copyright © 2018 Jane Oakley-Lohm

All rights reserved worldwide.

No part of the book may be copied or changed in any format, sold, or used in a way other than what is outlined in this book, under any circumstances, without the prior written permission of the publisher.

Publisher:
ASPG (Australian Self Publishing Group)
P.O. Box 159, Calwell, ACT Australia 2905
Email: publishaspg@gmail.com
http://www.inspiringpublishers.com

National Library of Australia Cataloguing-in-Publication entry

Author: Oakley-Lohm, Jane

Title: **My Buddy and Me: Normalising Grief and Loss & Learning Resilience/** *Jane Oakley-Lohm.*

Age group 5/8 Picture book

Illustrations hand drawn: Phyllis Nicoll

Graphic Design by Surendra Gupta

ISBN: 978-0-6483177-6-0

Genre Self Help

Dedicated to:

Laura and Regina, my children,
who like me have learnt resilience
when our roads were rough, but we all got through.

I have written this book to help build
resilience for all the children of the world,
as we are one community.

Special thanks to:

Phyllis Nicoll my mentor throughout
my counselling career.
&
Mother Earth for showing me resilience.

Jane and Phyllis met in Alice Springs and both
now reside in opposites ends of Tasmania Australia.

"Imagination is more important than knowledge.
For knowledge is limited to all we now know and understand,
while imagination embraces the entire world,
hence stimulating progress forward".

Albert Einstein

*To get anything done, you need to imagine it first.
Yes, anything. Once it is imagined, then you can take
the steps to accomplish goals.*

You can't accomplish a single solitary thing without imagination. You may have knowledge to make a mud brick but you need an imagination to build a town, you may also know that you need a pot, soil, water and a seed to grow a plant, but you need an imagination to make a garden.

Once you have an imagination to make a town or garden you can move forward to accomplish this, with this you have a purpose and there is no loss with a purpose. With an imagination and purpose you too can be successful.

"My buddy and me"

Normalising Loss and Grief
and learning resilience

Age group 5/8 Picture book
Author: Jane Oakley-Lohm
Grief and Loss counsellor and trainer
Illustrations hand drawn: **Phyllis Nicoll**
Retired Grief and Loss counsellor and trainer

Hello my name is Al.

What is your name?

I like to have fun, I like to play ball, board games, dance, swim, but on some days I feel sad.

Do you have days when you feel sad?

What do you do when you are sad?

When I'm a bit sad I like to go
in the garden or look out the window
to see the trees or birds and
look at the colours of the sky.
Sometimes I imagine an animal
or a surprise from the clouds.
I have seen a dog, tiger, plane,
a face, tree, rabbit, train and many more things. When
I'm sad I like to think that what ever I can see in the
clouds is looking down and looking after me.

What have you seen in the clouds?

I want to introduce my thumbprint "Buddy" to you. Buddy travels with me all the time. Buddy goes to school with me, shopping, on the bus or in the car. To the beach, play sports, walks, bike rides and Buddy is with me when I sleep.

Buddy can be a car, a cat, a rat, a flying mat, an elephant, an emu, a duck, a rocket, but today Buddy is a mouse.

Today I'm going to share a story about a walk I did in the garden.

When I was walking around the garden I was asking myself a lot of questions like………

What can you see
when you look at this tree?

Buddy says I can see leaves, branches, twigs, bark.

What colours do you think the tree may have?

Buddy says I think the tree would have the colour green.

Buddy says can you think of any more?

What would the tree roots look like that are under the ground?

Buddy says perhaps like roads?

What do the roots of the tree do?

Feeds the tree,
to make it grow taller says Buddy.

How would I look after the tree?

Keep topping up with water and fertiliser says Buddy.

What does the tree need to make it grow?

Mmmm says Buddy it would need sun, water, good soil.

What happens if a tree has a dead branch?

**That's easy says Buddy.
It will fall off one day and
a new shoot may grow in its place.**

Do you think the whole tree will stop growing if a branch has died?

No says Buddy.

Do you think the other branches will stop growing?

No says Buddy.

Do you think the other leaves will stop growing?

No says Buddy.

Do you think the roots will stop growing?

No says Buddy.

When the dead branch dies will it fall to the ground?

Yes says Buddy.

Do you think its possible that part of that branch that is left will reshoot again?

Yes says Buddy.

Do you think the tree would know when it has lost a branch?

Yes says Buddy.

Is this a loss for the tree?

Yesssss says Buddy.

I wondered what a loss could be for me?

Buddy said: Well I guess it could be: Loss of friendship, not being invited to a party, no one to play with, someone who may of died, a animal that may have died, being sick and can't play, a friend moving away, moving schools, family fights/separations at home, my plant dying and not getting that last piece of chocolate cake!!!!

Buddy said: Would you feel sad when you lost these things?

Yes I said

Would your body stop growing?

No I said

Would your hair stop growing?

No I said

Would your nails stop growing?

No I said

Would you stop moving?
No I said

Would you stop talking?
MMM Maybe for awhile

Could you still eat?
Yes

Buddy looks at me and says.

What little things can you do to make yourself happy for the day?

Well I could talk to someone, mum, dad, brother, sister, auntie, uncle, grandma, granddad, teachers, school counsellor, trusted friends. I could have a long bath, go for a walk in the garden, play a game, play with my pets, make a drawing, write a story, or go for a bike ride.

Buddy said: How can you help someone else when they are sad?

Listen to them, sit with them and invite them to play,

draw together,

go for a bike ride, talk to

an adult and let them know that your friend is sad.

I said to Buddy, have a good look at the tree; does the tree have a dead branch or twig?

Yes-said Buddy.

Is the rest of the tree growing?

Yes

Do you think the roots are still growing if the tree is growing?

Yes

Is the tree still living?

Yes

Will the dead branch/twig fall off the tree one day?

Yes

Will the tree still keep growing taller if this branch twig falls off?

Yes

Sometimes when we have been sad we have to be kind and nurture ourselves.

(The word nurture means taking care of yourself or other people.)

Just like the tree does when it loses a branch, before it reshoots it nurtures itself and then one day it will start to grow a new shoot in a different direction.

The tree is showing us that sometimes we lose things and we might be sad, but just like the tree if we nurture ourselves we will keep growing and going forward.

What can you do to help yourself to feel happy?

Give a pet a hug.

Read a book.

Put on some music.

Have a relaxing bath.

Have a dance.

Build a sand castle.

Go for a bike ride.

Play ball.

Do a drawing.

Go for a walk with a friend.

Get someone to help you write your thoughts down.

Talk to a friend.

What is the name of your thumbprint?

Who will your thumbprint be tomorrow?

Well....... well ....that was a busy day for us,
it's time to get cosy and snuggle up in bed.

You never know who Buddy maybe in the morning
maybe a star that shines bright.

Night night says Buddy I'm very tired and I have to go to sleep and get ready for another adventure tomorrow.

A gift from Jane:

https://youtu.be/r2cZNeRm7jg

About the Author

Jane has researched how some traditional old cultures of the world have dealt with grief and loss and then looked at how many people in the western world deal with their losses. People from many old cultures work through loss with a strategy which is different around the world but they seem to work through the loss with community support. Many people in the western world work through a loss without a strategy nor community support.

Jane wondered if you could design a strategy for people without community support would there be less compounding grief and loss and maybe less depression?

Jane lived in Central Australia for 30 years. When you walk in the desert there is no noise, people or distractions but there is so much to learn from Mother Earth.

Jane went onto to develop a strategy that can be used for the many people around the world that are losing their community and culture support and for people that never had it.

The strategy and tool is based on what Jane believes is shown to us from Mother Earth. "A tree." Jane has been using her visual tool for many years in counselling and now takes this knowledge to train others.

Cut Outs for Your Rooms

Cut Outs for Your Rooms

www.ingramcontent.com/pod-product-compliance
Lightning Source LLC
Chambersburg PA
CBHW041714290426
44110CB00024B/2830